**WAITING UNTIL
THE FUR FLIES
YOUR WAY:
A MASCOT MEMOIR**

BELAYED
GRATIFICATION

BY DAVID STOGDILL

ISBN: 978-1-943258-76-5

Edited by: Elizabeth Russell

Published by Warren Publishing
Charlotte, NC
www.warrenpublishing.net
Printed in the United States

*This book is dedicated to my loving wife, Lyndsey,
and daughter, Lacey. You both are my
rock and reason for everything. #stoggystyle!*

*To my sisters Yvonne and Aoi (Joyce).
Yvonne helped me get my first mascot gig.*

*To The Charlotte Mascot Crew. (Brett, Allison,
Miguel, Sarah, Ken, KC, Lee, Gina, Emily, Caroline,
Hoff, Ryan, Misty, Chris E., Jenn, Chris R., and Jessica).*

You all have always been my local family.

TABLE OF CONTENTS

INTRODUCTION

MY CAREER PATH as a professional mascot began in college. While this occupation is certainly one of the most unique and obscure lines of work that anyone can choose, it is also one of the most fulfilling and amazing careers you could ever imagine. When people found out what I did for a living, there was always an array of questions. My answers to these questions:

- ✓ Yes, it's a real job.
- ✓ Yes, it's full-time.
- ✓ Yes, I can make a living at it, but no, I am not going to tell you how much I make.
- ✓ Yes, I work in the off-season.
- ✓ No, I don't hang out with the players.
- ✓ Yes, I have met Michael Jordan.
- ✓ No, I cannot hook you up with tickets.
- ✓ Yes, I know the cheerleaders. In fact, I married one.
- ✓ And, finally, **YES, IT'S HOT IN THERE!**

The best way I can describe my career path is to compare it to that of a professional athlete. Don't get me wrong here ... I didn't make the salary of a professional athlete. But I made enough to live on. I spent over twenty years as a mascot. I started out in college, then went to the minor leagues, and finally became a pro. I moved to new teams in new cities and traveled the world. My career followed what looks like a familiar path of a professional athlete. College to the minor leagues (Arena Football) and then to the pros. I spent two years as Butch the Cougar at Washington State University, then a year as Scorch the Dragon for the Portland Forest Dragons, an Arena Football League team. After that, I moved to the National Football League, serving as Blitz the Seahawk for the Seattle Seahawks for four years. Next came a year in Japan as the mascot for a professional baseball team in the city of Hiroshima.

Returning home, I rejoined the NFL, spending a year and a half as Sir Purr, mascot of the Carolina Panthers. And finally, I landed my dream job with the National Basketball Association, spending nine years as Rufus Lynx, mascot of the Charlotte Bobcats.

At the end of the 2014-2015 season, I hung up the fur. The Charlotte Bobcats officially changed their name back to the Charlotte Hornets, and I decided it was time for a change. That's my mascot career in a nutshell. It was filled with ups and downs, blood and sweat, fur and feathers.

While I was in college, I didn't just attend football games in a fur suit. I actually graduated with a bachelor's degree in sociology and a teaching certificate in elementary education. But once I found out that people could actually make a living as professional mascots, I decided to take my shot. I figured that if I didn't make it to the big leagues, then I would fall back on my education and become a teacher. This is where I adopted my pro-athlete mentality. My plan

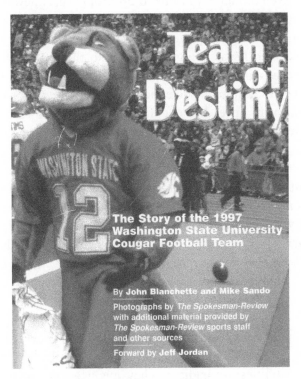

Team of Destiny

The Story of the 1997 Washington State University Cougar Football Team

By John Blanchette and Mike Sando

Photographs by *The Spokesman-Review* with additional material provided by *The Spokesman-Review* sports staff and other sources

Forward by Jeff Jordan

My first magazine cover. The WSU Cougars hadn't played in the Rose Bowl Game since 1931—a sixty-seven year absence. This was a historic year for the Cougars.

was to start off in college, go to the minor leagues, then make it to the pros.

My mother was a very traditional Japanese woman who always asked me, "Why do you do this job? Why do you wear that silly costume? You need to do what you went to school for and be a teacher. A teacher is a respectable profession."

Even though my mother didn't approve, I knew that I had a calling and decided to go the unconventional route; I wanted to wear fur and follow my dreams. I decided I was going to make it to the professional level as a mascot, one way or another. However, I also knew that literacy and education would always be my platform. Instead of encouraging students to read as a teacher, I could do it as a mascot. I knew a mascot has a lot of influence on children. With this power, I could not only influence how they perceived the team, but also how they perceived literacy. I had the chance to make a difference. I always thought that if a little boy or girl who didn't like to read saw that the giant furry, funny mascot does like to read ... well, then maybe they might pick up a book. Then eventually, if they made reading a daily habit, they could catch the reading bug. Reading can open the eyes and minds of children and lead them to new horizons. Then you never know what might happen. They could become anything they want because with reading, the possibilities are endless. They might grow up to be the next president, a Nobel Prize winner, or a scientist who cures cancer. Reading opens children's minds to endless possibilities, exposing them to new things they might never have imagined were possible.

The purpose of this book is to make you smile, encourage you not to take yourself too seriously, and to be patient because things don't always go the way you want them to. The little movie that plays in your head doesn't always run the way you expect. If you are patient and can hang in there, then maybe, one day, *the fur will fly your way*.

CHAPTER 1
Belayed and Delayed

IN 2008, as the end of the NBA season approached, the Charlotte Bobcats were on the verge of their first playoff berth in team history. When a sports franchise makes the post-season playoffs, the city often becomes electric with excitement, and the entertainment value of the games rises significantly. For our first playoff game, the game day entertainment staff had been told to bring their A-games. High-profile halftime acts and national recording artists were brought in to perform and sing the national anthem. The in-house entertainment teams worked on their best routines.

I also made sure my best fur was ready to go. Because of the ramp-up in entertainment, team introductions were taken to another level ... literally. As a part of team introductions, Rufus was to be taken to the upper levels of the rafters and lowered down using a belay—a system of ropes and pulleys. This was the first time the mascot had been allowed to perform a big, over-the-top stunt. I was slightly nervous, because I have a small fear of heights. Out of costume, heights tended to make me nervous, with sweaty palms, and butterflies in my stomach. In costume, however, I became Superman! I could do anything. I could rappel from the rafters, jump from an airplane, or drive a race car at 200 miles an hour. Needless to say, I was ready to do this. Once I put on my costume head, I made a mental switch, becoming invincible. When I flipped that switch and became Rufus Lynx, Bobcats mascot, nothing could stop me. I was no longer the introverted quiet guy. I became the crazy, thrill-seeking, fun-loving, bright orange mascot who danced with the fans and made everyone laugh. The thrill-seeking part of my character definitely came out of its shell when I went into the costume.

The week before our first game was filled with rehearsals. Video, lighting, audio, dance routines, comedy bits, skits to be performed during time outs, contests, and halftime acts ... you name it. Every single aspect of the entire game had to be perfect. The entire script of the game was pored over, and full dress rehearsals were scheduled, even for the mascot. This meant multiple hours in full costume while all aspects of the game-day experience were tested, run through, and perfected. For the mascot belay, we hired Aerial Concepts, a company that specializes in mascot stunts, belaying, and rappelling. The owner of the company is a former professional mascot, which made me feel more comfortable with the arrangement.

Every single aspect of an NBA game involves entertainment. The entire event outside of the actual play on the court is scripted for the viewing pleasure of the fans. This takes a tremendous amount of planning and practice to execute. When it was time to practice team introductions, I was taken to the very top rafters of Time Warner Cable Arena. Safety equipment was strapped on over my costume. I wore a team jersey over the harness to hide it from view of the audience. It was secured so that I could be lowered in an upright position. The rope was attached at the top of my shoulder blades behind my head, feet dangling below. I was directed to the step-off point and instructed to get into position to wait for our cue. This meant climbing over the railing of the catwalk and hanging about 150 feet in the air while music and timing were perfected below.

Even though I had my internal "costume courage" on, that first step onto the railing was definitely a challenge. With each step up the railing, the adrenaline rushed in. I swung my leg over the rail and looked down. The court looked tiny below me. I couldn't believe I was doing this willingly. I realized that if something were to happen to this rope ...

Rufus Lynx seen here in a "Reverse Belay". Started from the court, raised to the rafters ... upside down as the banner prompts fans to cheer!

that would be the end. In that instant, I mentally took a step back and looked at my life a little differently. When a person puts themselves in a situation such as rappelling from an extreme height, it can make them think and take stock of their life. All the trivial things in life instantly become insignificant when faced with the possibility of falling to your death.

I felt the rope and harness tighten as I eased my weight into the straps, then let go of the railing. My stomach bottomed out. Butterflies hit the bottom of my spine with a punch. I felt like the butterflies then grabbed my soul, traveled up my spine, and seized my breath. Slowly, I was lowered to about twenty feet below the cat walk. With each second that passed, I felt like my pounding heart was going to explode. I stopped about eye level with the top of the scoreboard. This was where I was to wait for the break in music that signaled Rufus's grand entrance. My life literally hung in the balance.

As I dangled there, the introduction video played, dancers went into position, the spot light was at the ready, and those pesky butterflies performed somersaults in my stomach. I took a deep breath. Blew out. Another deep breath, blew out again. Each breath filled up the inside of the mask with condensation. Fog formed on the inside of the signature Rufus sunglasses, leaving my view of the stadium fuzzy. I realized the music was reaching the point that signaled the start of my descent. I tensed, waiting for the drop.

Suddenly, the game operations director yelled, "Hold it! Cut!" I knew instantly that something down below had gone wrong: the timing of the dancers, or the video, or who knew what. There I was, suspended in mid-air, hanging there. Just waiting. I yelled to my belay man, "Hey, what's going on? What do we do now?" His response: "I was told to just hold on and wait a minute."

I thought, "Seriously? Am I supposed to just dangle here 150 feet above the court at the top of the arena?"

The answer was yes. What was supposed to be a few minutes became five, then ten, then fifteen minutes ... I just hung there. As the minutes ticked by, the butterflies slowly dissipated and eventually disappeared. There was no reason to get angry or more stressed ... I had no control of the rope. The belay company made sure that I was completely safe. I couldn't do anything about it except hang out. My mind wandered. I realized that this event could serve as a parallel of my life and career. Maybe I had to wait a while before things could go my way, which in this case was straight down. As sweat dripped down the middle of my back, I thought maybe if I just hang in there and stick it out, things might swing my way.

There are defining moments and events in everyone's lives that cause them to either rise to the occasion or fall flat. I have experienced both. When I experience the latter, I try my hardest not to dwell on it. If I am patient and learn to laugh at myself, maybe I can learn from it. I try not to take myself too seriously and figure out the best way to recover and move on. There are moments you can prepare for and moments that catch you by surprise ...

 **THIS WAS ONE OF THOSE MOMENTS.
I HUNG IN MID-AIR.
HOW WOULD I REDEEM MYSELF?**

CHAPTER 2
Pro Debut

WORKING AS A MASCOT in college was ... well, there's no other way to put it: it was a blast. I had the opportunity to perform in cities and states around the country. I competed in the NCA (National Cheerleading Association) College Mascot Competition in Daytona Beach, Florida. My college mascot experience culminated in a performance at the Rose Bowl in Pasadena, California. These are experiences that I will always look back on with great fondness.

I enjoyed my college mascot days so much that when I learned it was possible to be a professional mascot, that it was a real job and career, I decided right then and there that's what I wanted to do. "That is all me!" I thought. My plan? To progress from the college level to the minor leagues and then to the pros.

My first step was to make sure I was prepared for tryouts. I didn't know where or when that would be, but I knew I needed to be ready the moment an opportunity presented itself. I knew that most teams were looking for creativity, athletic ability, and rhythm.

And I knew I needed to be unique enough in my abilities that I stood out among the other applicants. So I worked on building the skills that teams would be looking for in an ideal candidate. I took tumbling lessons, hip-hop dance classes, and even American Sign Language. I took ASL because mascots aren't supposed to speak when in costume, and this gave me a way to communicate. My plan was to build my resume and expand my skill set. I saw each new skill as a feather in my cap. Each feather prepared

Scorch the Dragon. Arena Football League, Portland Forest Dragons. My first pro gig!

me to be the best performer that I could be. Dancing equaled a feather. Tumbling—another feather. Even some typical resume items like "experience working with kids" equaled a feather.

I landed my first paid mascot job as "Scorch the Dragon" for the Portland Forest Dragons, an Arena Football League (AFL) team. Scorch was my first stepping stone on my way to the pros. The AFL is

My family with Scorch. Pictured from left to right: my sister (Yvonne), my mom (Hideko), my father (George), and my sister (Aoi, also called Joyce).

considered the minor league to the NFL, but since this was an actual paying job, I felt it was my professional mascot debut.

I was doing my student teaching at an elementary school in my home town of Lacey, Washington. However, Portland was only a three-hour drive, so I could easily drive down for the weekend and work the game. The team knew my commute, so they provided a hotel room for me to stay in after the game. As a college kid, I could not envision a cooler gig. I could hang out in a new city, work a game, go out on the town, and then stay in a nice hotel. Not too shabby for my first pro mascot job.

Early on, I faced a challenging moment that quickly taught me about instantaneous redemption. One of those challenging moments came quickly. Would I rise to the occasion? Or would I fall flat on my face? The scene was opening night at the Rose

Garden Arena in Portland, Oregon. The first game of the season was also the first time that I had worn this particular mascot costume and it was definitely different from Butch The Cougar. Scorch was a scary, muscular dragon with a huge rubber and foam head.

I was excited and anxious for my first game as a professional mascot. I wanted to make sure everything was on point, so I had prepped properly and made sure that I was hydrated. Since it's so much hotter inside the suit, it's crucial to be well-hydrated on game days. Otherwise, muscle cramps can take you out of the game. The hydration process usually begins the day before, then continues the day of and the day after. Nerves raged inside of me, but the moment I put on the costume and strapped on my head, I made the mental switch to become fully engrossed in the character of Scorch.

I strutted to the entertainment tunnel with purpose. Sitting there primed and ready at the entrance of the production tunnel was the All-Terrain Vehicle I was to ride onto the field. As I mounted the four-wheeler, I felt the excitement build inside of me. The engine was already on, and I could feel it purring beneath me. The music began with a loud energy-building beat, the crowd began to murmur, the spotlights clicked on.

The scene played out like a movie. As the spotlight switched on, all other lights went out and there was a dramatic booming sound, followed by utter silence. Complete blackness surrounded the spotlight. I revved up the four-wheeler, and the production tunnel assistant gave me the thumbs up. I gunned the throttle and the ATV lurched forward. My entire body jerked as the ATV accelerated. It felt like I was flying onto the field. The weight of the costume head and torque of the engine cocked my head back and I held onto the handle bars for dear life. I could hear the wind blowing into the screen of the dragon's mouth, which was also my direct line of sight. It was a straight shot to the center of the field. I squeezed the brakes as hard as I could and came to a dramatic stop. I leaped onto the four-wheeler's seat, pumping my arms to get the crowd to cheer louder. My blood surged with the energy of the crowd, and I knew I needed to be as energetic as possible.

I leaped as high as I could into the air, landing on the field, and … BAM. My ankle folded like a lawn chair under the weight of my body, bending in a direction it wasn't supposed to. The pain was instant. I didn't think it was broken, but I knew something was wrong. I tried my best to ignore the pain and make it look like nothing happened. Since the adrenaline was pumping, I was able to keep performing despite the immense pain. Luckily, immediately after I jumped, there was another music cue and the dancers poured onto the field. Under cover of the dancers' entrance, I made my way back onto the four-wheeler and drove off the field. My ankle was so swollen and painful I could barely put weight on it. I was devastated. What was I going to do? How could I make this work?

THIS WAS MY MOMENT.
I HUNG IN MID-AIR.
HOW WOULD I REDEEM MYSELF?

I could walk, but I had a severe limp. The first thought that entered my head was that a limping mascot wasn't a very good look. My new bosses were not going to be impressed with their new performer. The doomsday scenario in my head was that my professional mascot career was over before it even started. Well, of course, I was being overly dramatic, but what do you expect? I was a man who was trying to make a living by dressing up in a dragon costume.

My solution? I figured out that I could disguise my limp to look like a serious strut. I was just trying not to put too much weight on my ankle. To the audience, however, it looked like I had a mad swagger! I worked the entire game with a pimp-like strut, and absolutely no one knew that I had sprained my ankle.

The show must go on.

CHAPTER 3
The Big Leagues

SOON AFTER MY FIRST YEAR in the AFL, the Seattle Seahawks announced they were launching a brand new character. Tryouts for performers were coming soon. This was my chance to make it to the National Football League! This meant full-time work with benefits, and my first real job out of college.

I grew up near the Seattle area and as a kid, watched the Seahawks play. I was a huge fan. From the time that I was six years old, I was convinced that I was going to play professional football in the NFL as a Seahawks player. I didn't even have to think about other careers as I was growing up because football player was my choice. However, as I moved from Little League football to middle and then high school football, reality set in. The fact that I was 5'5" and 135 pounds soaking wet as a senior in high school meant that college scouts were not knocking on my door to offer any Division I scholarships.

This job audition for the Seahawks' official team mascot was my chance to make it to the NFL in my own way. This was my dream. If I got the job, it would mean that I would be on the field during a Seahawks game as part of the team, and I would be wearing a Seahawks uniform. Never mind that my uniform would include a beak and feathers.

As part of my preparations for the Seahawks tryouts, I decided to take beginning tumbling lessons. This was one of my strategies to set myself apart from the other applicants. If I could tumble, maybe I could outshine the other candidates. In my hometown of Lacey, Washington, there was only one gymnastics facility. So naturally, this is where I went to learn how to tumble. At that time, they didn't have any adult tumbling classes. I knew that I had to learn, so I didn't take no for an answer. I asked if I could take a beginner's class anyway.

Amazingly, the answer was yes. I was allowed to be a part of the children's classes. I was the only adult and the only guy in a class full of little girls ranging in age from six to twelve. The tumblers in the class all giggled and laughed at me when I walked in that first day. I had to swallow my pride, suck it up, and learn. Needless to say, it was pretty awkward in the beginning. But, over time, the girls became my friends and even began to give me pointers. By the time of the tryouts for Seahawks mascot, I had learned a very rough round off and the beginnings of a back handspring. I just had not actually landed one yet.

I was almost ready, but my preparation time was up. It was time for the tryouts. The team had received

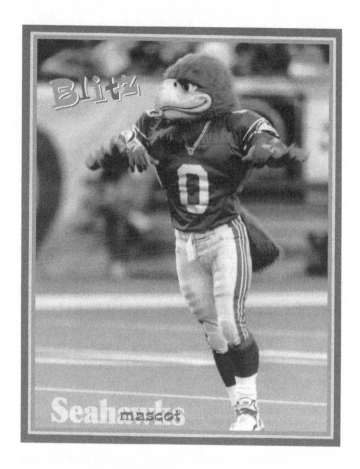

resumes and highlight videos from around the country. From this pool of candidates, they chose the top ten best applicants. The location of the tryouts was a local high school gym located near the Seahawks practice facility. Next to the gym was a classroom that became the waiting room for the top ten applicants. We all sat around talking to each other and secretly sizing each other up. Since I had some college and arena football mascot experience, I had made the cut into the top ten and earned the right to be sitting in the classroom. There were some other applicants with professional mascot experience, so I knew the competition was stiff. Our instructions during the tryout portion of the auditions were to show what I had always heard to be the three gold standard traits of a good mascot: creativity, athletic ability, and rhythm.

We started with a formal interview. Walking into the gym, I faced a panel of judges seated at desks in a semi-circle around one chair. I lowered myself into the chair, feeling like a suspect in an old detective movie. The pressure was on. The interrogation team, I mean the judges, consisted of ten people, including the director of the dance team, vice president of marketing, vice president of community relations, and a number of other executives and front office staff members.

**THIS WAS MY MOMENT.
I HUNG IN MID-AIR.
WOULD I RISE TO THE OCCASION?
OR FALL FLAT ON MY FACE?**

During the interview, one of the questions was: "Do you know how to tumble?" How to respond? I paused and finally said, "Yes, absolutely! I know how to tumble." I spoke in a confident manner, giving them no clue to the uncertainty that I felt. The sweat dripped down my forehead and another drop inched down my spine.

This wasn't a complete lie, I told myself; it was just a little exaggeration. When the interview process was complete, we moved to the tryout portion. I had an audio cassette tape prepared. (It was the nineties. Yes, we used audio cassettes.) The tape was exactly three minutes long, filled with different cuts of music. I planned to try and hit all aspects of what they were looking for. I had a skit to show creativity, plus a dance routine with high energy dance moves and excitement to show rhythm. As I finished up my dance routine, I realized I needed to show them that I had told the truth in my interview … that I could tumble.

At the last moment, I decided to throw in my sad attempt at a round off leading to a back handspring. It was all or nothing. My adrenaline took over and with as much power that I could muster, I leaped into the air and went into my run. I decided to rely on everything that my tumbling coach and the little girls in my class had taught me. I executed and landed my first tumbling pass to end the routine.

The team took around two and a half months to make their decision. It felt like the longest summer of my life. The days dragged on and on. But I didn't sit around. I continued to take tumbling lessons and learned to accomplish additional tumbling moves.

Finally, I received the fateful phone call. I was offered the job of Blitz, the official mascot for the Seattle Seahawks. By the time my first game rolled around, my skills had expanded. I could walk on my hands across the end zone, complete multiple backhand springs (vs. a single one), and confidently throw a standing back tuck, which is a back flip with no hands from a standing position. I had risen to the occasion at tryouts and was now proving to the Seahawks that they made the right choice. Now that I officially made it to the NFL, I knew that I had to continue to learn and become a better mascot. I knew that I had to continue to put additional feathers in my cap.

CHAPTER 4
Touchdown Catch from a Legend

ONE OF THE GREAT PERKS of working in the NFL as a mascot was the opportunity to go to the Pro Bowl in Hawaii. For many years in the early 2000s, the NFL held the Pro Bowl in Hawaii every year. The NFL would bring multiple mascots and cheerleaders from around the league to make appearances and perform at the game. This was an entire week of high profile appearances and events, including the NFL Skills Challenge, Community Relations Events, and Special Olympics with players, just to name a few. Many of these events were shown on TV and ESPN, giving teams—and mascots—national exposure.

One of the larger events mascots participated in was the Alumni Beach Bowl. This was a flag football game on Waikiki Beach in Honolulu between retired football legends. Roger Craig, Norman "Boomer" Esiason, Billy "White Shoes" Johnson, and Jerry Rice were among the retired athletes playing in the game. The teams were divided by NFC and AFC— the National Football Conference vs. the American

Football Conference. It was a typical Hawaiian summer day: ninety degrees, ninety-five percent humidity, and even hotter on the beach with the sun's rays reflecting off the sand and water.

One of the things about being a mascot most people don't realize is that on average, it's thirty to forty degrees warmer inside a costume versus outside. So, all the mascots felt like they were on the verge of heat stroke and exhaustion. Lots of water and sports drinks were needed to cool off. But, as always, the show must go on.

1998 Rose Bowl. Washington State Cougars vs. Michigan Wolverines. Butch T. Cougar taking it all in.

I knew from experience how important it is to stay hydrated as a mascot. I had learned the hard way the consequences of when you are not as prepared as you should be. While I was in college at Washington State University, I was team mascot for the 1998 season, an amazing year to be the mascot for a national powerhouse collegiate football team. The Cougars were heading to the Rose Bowl to take on the University of Michigan Wolverines. The Cougars were led by top NFL prospect quarterback Ryan Leaf, who was predicted to go either number one or two in the next year's NFL draft (Payton Manning was the other top college quarterback of that year). The Michigan Wolverines were led by quarterback Brian Griese and Heisman Trophy winner Charles Woodson. The Rose Bowl in Pasadena, California, is one of the biggest college games of the year. Along with the team, the entire band, the cheerleaders, and the team mascot traveled for this game. Southern California is typically known for warm weather, even on January first. As the game went on, the Cougar costume grew heavier and heavier, soaked by sweat as I gave it my all. I ran up and down the sidelines, clapped and danced as hard as I could. This was the biggest game of my career, and I wanted to make sure that everyone who saw Butch the Cougar knew it.

Second quarter came around and I ran out of gas. I mistakenly thought that I had consumed enough water the day before and morning of the game. I was flat out wrong. The heat overwhelmed me, and my vision blurred. Nausea set in and I had to get off of the field and away from the sidelines. I sprinted to the tunnel and ducked inside. About halfway up, I fell to my knees and began to vomit. However, I had nothing in my system to throw up, so I just dry heaved. I lifted the Cougar head barely enough to get my mouth clear of the fur neck flap. However, from the vantage point of the front of the tunnel, all fans could see was the cougar ... on his hands and knees ... arching his back ... convulsing like he was about to throw up. I looked like a giant cat with a hair ball. And that's how I knew how important it was to stay hydrated on the hot sandy beaches of Hawaii.

My sister, Yvonne, helped me get my first gig as a mascot that led to a career. She was a WSU Cheerleader.

Late in the fourth quarter of the Alumni Beach bowl, the NFC marched down the field (or beach) with the legendary Joe Theismann as quarterback. I could see that the action was nearing one end of the field, so I decided to position myself behind the end zone. I knew that TV cameras would be panning my direction as the players attempted to score.

During one of the final plays of the game, Thiesmann dropped back to pass. He was scanning for an open wide receiver in the end zone. The defensive lineman rushed after him for the sack. Thiesmann moved to his right to avoid the defensive player coming at him. As he threw the ball, he released a perfect spiral to the back of the end zone.

**THIS WAS MY MOMENT.
I HUNG IN MID-AIR.
WOULD I RISE TO THE OCCASION
OR FALL FLAT ON MY FACE.**

I sprinted behind the receiver, still behind the end zone and not on the field itself. I could tell Thiesmann had overthrown the ball slightly. I knew that even if the receiver did catch the ball, it would be funny for fans to see the mascot attempting a dive for the catch. I watched as the ball sailed over the outstretched hands of the receiver and out of the end zone. I was in the right place at the right time. I dove as far and high as I could, and my body became parallel with the sand.

The ball hit my hands in mid-air and somehow safely stayed in the grip of my feathered gloves (or wings).

I made the catch! I landed on my chest and stomach with the ball securely in my wings. Sand flew all over my beak and feathers. The crowd roared. I jumped up and performed a touch down dance like Billy "White Shoes" Johnson, and spiked the ball as hard as I could. Over the loud speaker, the announcer exclaimed: "Oh my goodness, Blitz the Seahawk with the spectacular catch in the back of the end zone!"

Later that night, I saw Joe Theismann in the lobby of the hotel. I approached him and introduced myself. I was out of costume, so I told him who I was and that I was on the beach with him earlier that day. He shook my hand and said, "Oh, that was you? Wow, that was a spectacular catch you made!"

Having grown up a football fan, I was in awe. The fact that I was on the field interacting with football greats and legends in the paradise of Hawaiian Paradise was truly amazing. And on top of that, I am one of a select group of people in the history of the game of football who can truthfully say, "I caught a touchdown pass thrown by the great Joe Theismann."

This particular Pro Bowl was also where I first met my wife, Lyndsey. She was coordinating a group of cheerleaders who were performing at half time of the Pro Bowl. One of the events she attended was a pregame pep rally. We even performed a stunt together, although I was in costume as Blitz. I was performing with a number of other NFL mascots; however,

It was love at first sight...of feathers. This was the first time that I met my wife. (Even though I was in costume and was not allowed to speak.) I am standing on Lyndsey's right leg in our first photo together. It was not until years later when we met again in Charlotte out of costume, that we realized we had previously (and fatefully) met in Hawaii.

oddly enough, she only had pictures of my character. I believe it was my moves and body language that caught her eye! Years later, we met for a second time in Charlotte.

In September of 2004, Lyndsey had been in Charlotte for just a few months and worked as a director of operations for a large cheerleading company. One of her main roles with this company was an event planner, and one particular event she produced was called *Spirit of Hope*. This event was a cheerleading exhibition and fundraiser benefiting the March Forth with Hope Foundation. The Foundation was established earlier that year in honor of Hope

Stout, a young Charlotte girl who lost her battle with Osteosarcoma in January of that year. The March Forth with Hope Foundation provides financial assistance to families who have children battling life-threatening illnesses or injuries. As part of the entertainment for the day, Lyndsey hired local pro mascots and pro dance teams to perform. I was one of those characters and when we met, I instantly felt a connection. I still remember what she was wearing that day. It was a long khaki skirt and yellow polo shirt (super sexy event planner attire!). Throughout the event, she came to the locker rooms to check in on the performers. She would ask if we had enough water, Gatorade, towels, etc. Later, she would admit that she made up excuses to see and talk to me.

Pre game photo with Hope Stout (on my left) and her best friend, Emily.

At that time, she was also captain of the NBA Charlotte Bobcats' interactive stunt squad, the Rally Cats. Along with being a professional mascot in Charlotte, I worked as the mascot assistant during these NBA games. The Rally Cats were a professional co-ed cheerleading team who led cheers, performed stunts, and tumbled during the Bobcats games. They were a separate entertainment team from the dancers who were known as the Lady Cats. Lyndsey and I saw each other at one of the games and instantly recognized one another. We had reconnected, and we continued to talk and flirt throughout the season.

One Friday night after a big game, Charlotte's night life was active and bustling. All of the dancers and cheerleaders were out on the town, and one particular club in Uptown Charlotte was packed to capacity. A number of local celebrities were hanging out in the VIP area. As expected, the dancers and cheerleaders were included in this exclusive section of the balcony. The level with the dance floor and main bar was down below, where the common folk (AKA me) spent their time. Lyndsey was in the VIP area talking with a large local celebrity. (She says they were just talking. However, I think that he was buying her drinks and hitting on her. But, we have different versions of the story and for this story, we will refer to him as "Mr. Anonymous"). At around this time, I entered the club. I, of course, didn't have VIP access, so my friend and I were circling the dance floor.

As the night went on, additional drinks were consumed, and the club swelled with people. Lyndsey was still up in the balcony talking with this local celebrity. Then, it happened! She noticed me from high above and instantly turned to Mr. Anonymous and said, "Thank you for the conversation, but I am sorry, I have to go see about a guy." She had actually taken the big line from the movie *Good Will Hunting* and used it to pursue me. She left the balcony and came

Pre-game photo with Hope and Stuart Stout during the incredible 2003 Super Bowl season.

down to see me amongst the peasants. We ended up dancing together until the wee hours of the morning.

On our second date, we stayed in and rented the movie *Fifty First Dates*. This movie is shot on location in Honolulu, Hawaii. As we watched the movie and were getting to know each other, we realized we had first met in Hawaii at the Pro Bowl. She even had the photos to prove it. Over a decade of marriage later, we are now parents to a beautiful, talented, smart little girl named Lacey Caroline and often refer to her as our "Hope" baby. After all, Hope Stout's spirit and the foundation enabled us to reconnect in Charlotte. The rest, as they say, is history.

CHAPTER 5

International Man of Fur

A **FTER MY TIME** with Seattle Seahawks, I packed my bags and headed to Japan. I landed a job as the mascot for a professional baseball team in the city of Hiroshima. The team posted their job to an American mascot job website in hopes of providing an international experience for a young American. Their ideal candidate would be a college graduate with some mascot experience who was willing to move to Japan. The reason for the overseas search was that the owner of the team had spent part of his college career in America attending the University of California—Berkeley. He had such a good time and made such great friends in America that he wanted to give a young American the opportunity to come to Japan and experience the people, the food, and the culture of his home country.

The next move in my mascot career was to take this opportunity and live my life to the fullest. I could not think of a better way to do this and get paid for it. I was relatively young and had no attachments here in the States. Although my mother is Japanese, the Japanese language was not something that I had mastered. I could only speak a few words of the language but was eager to learn. The team provided round-trip plane tickets at the beginning of the contract, during Christmas time, and at the end. They also arranged for me to live in the team dorm. I bought a bike for about the equivalent of twenty dollars that I rode to and from the stadium. It was right in the heart of downtown Hiroshima across the street from Peace Park, located at the center of the atomic bomb detonation during World War II.

The experience was incredibly amazing. Baseball is essentially the national sport in Japan. The fans are dedicated, passionate, and love their baseball and animated characters. I took it all in. I met new people and experienced new foods. I loved performing for the Japanese fans, who laughed and enjoyed my crazy antics and dance moves.

One of the best things about working as a professional mascot for any team is wearing the uniform and actually going onto the field. When the baseball team was playing at home for several games in a row, called a home stand, they warmed up hours prior to the start of the game. Batting practice was a key component of this. To my delight, I was allowed to join the bat boys in the outfield to catch fly balls. I was amazed, and truly could not believe that this was happening. I grew up playing little league sports, baseball included. So, like all little boys, I dreamed of playing the big leagues. As a kid, I pretended I was a world-famous baseball player and even practiced a quick sloppy version of my autograph. I was sure it would one day be scribbled on my very own baseball card or a box of Wheaties. I imagined hitting home runs and even robbing home runs off batters at the wall with a leaping catch. When I found out that I was allowed to catch fly balls during batting practice, I thought that this was my chance to live out my boyhood fantasy.

In my mind, I imagined I was an outfielder on a professional baseball field, playing against real pro baseball players. I grabbed my glove and ran onto the field. I smiled from ear to ear. I smelled the grass. I heard the crack of the bat. Baseball filled the air. I took it all in as I ran to get into position. I caught a few short fly balls, and the batting coaches shouted out pointers and tips in Japanese while the team interpreter translated. I loved it. I gained confidence as I made a few catches here and there. Suddenly, I heard the smack of the bat as the ball connected. I watched as it soared my way. I had visions of making the catch like one of the great outfielders—Ken Griffey Jr. or Bo Jackson, for example. I imagined myself running with huge strides and then backing up to the warning track. This was my chance to make an outstanding and athletic play as the ball headed toward the stands. It looked like a home run! I sprinted as fast as I could toward the wall, planning to leap up and grab the ball out of the air. I followed the ball through the air as it headed toward the stands. I was going to do it! The ball was coming closer and was about to go over the edge. At exactly the right moment, I jumped as high as I could and stretched my glove to make the grab ... when BAM. My glove was just a few inches off the mark and the ball nailed the top of wall, bounced back, and hit me directly in the eye. It began to swell instantly.

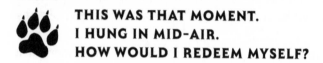 **THIS WAS THAT MOMENT.**
I HUNG IN MID-AIR.
HOW WOULD I REDEEM MYSELF?

Would I rise up and keep moving? Yes, I would go on to perform as a mascot at my first Japanese pro baseball game with a black eye. Luckily, no one could see under the mask. However, the entire area around my eye throbbed with pain the whole game.

The show must go on.

CHAPTER 6
Interpreter Out of Fur

I N JAPAN, mascots are expected to spend six days a week working in the team office wearing a suit and tie. I had truly become a "Salary Man," the term used for the millions of businessmen who fill the subways daily in Japan. I worked in the international department, and one of my responsibilities was to be a representative and ambassador for English-speaking visitors. I was one of only four people in the entire organization who spoke English. During the season, there were often visitors from other countries who toured the stadium or met with team representatives and executives. In one particular instance, a group of dignitaries and executive businessmen from Canada were visiting. One of my responsibilities was to take them on a tour of the stadium. When the team was on a home stand, the field was used for practice as well as games. I took the group through various parts of the stadium around the field, and we ended up in the stands behind home plate. Many of the players were on the field warming up, playing catch, and practicing.

I ushered the group to a specific spot, and we stopped to watch a few of the players in action. It was a nice day and the people on the tour were enjoying this behind-the-scenes look at the team and the field.

At this point in the season I knew most of the players, so I felt comfortable waving, shaking hands with, or fist bumping a player. The majority of the players didn't speak English. However, many Japanese people take a beginning English language course in school and can speak basic greetings or pleasantries.

Every Japanese team has a limit of four foreign players. The team's foreign players could be from anywhere in the world. However, many of these players were American and the team had an English interpreter as well. Inevitably, as players worked together and befriended each other, language exchanges occurred. One particular Japanese player on the team had only learned specific words in the English vernacular. As you may have guessed, he focused on the swear words.

The tour was going very well. The dignitaries were enjoying their time taking in the sights and sounds of baseball. It was a perfect day for a stroll around the stadium. The sun was out, and a slight breeze filled the air. Then the player who spoke only these colorful English words spotted me from the outfield. He smiled, waved, and then yelled at the top of his lungs to greet me. "Hey ****-sucker! Hey mother-******! How you doing?" I was flabbergasted. Some of the members of the group snickered and laughed.

I was so embarrassed, I instantly ushered the group out of the stands to another part of the stadium. My face turned completely red and I just waved and ducked my head, all the while trying to get the visiting dignitaries out of there as fast as I could. I would definitely say I gave this group an unforgettable tour!

Japanese Pro Baseball Mascots! My character was designed by the same company who made the Philly Phanatic (second mascot from the left.)

CHAPTER 7
Welcome to North Carolina

ALTHOUGH I COULD have stayed longer, I decided to return to the States after a year. I moved back to the Seattle area, looked for work, and waited for my next tryout for a mascot gig. Even in college, I had dreamed of making it to the NBA as a mascot. In the mascot world, some consider the NBA as the pinnacle, and this was my ultimate goal. Little did I realize that my first crack at the NBA would come in the form of an audition with the Sacramento Kings. A good friend of mine, a former mascot for the San Francisco 49ers, was the In Arena Host for the Kings. He knew a lot of mascot performers around the country and was in charge of finding qualified applicants. I was one of those applicants. (The old adage, "It's not what you know, it's who you know," applied here.) In the years since I'd graduated from college, I had turned in many applications and highlight tapes to various NBA teams with mascot job openings, but never received an invite for a tryout. Now I had a friend on the inside, and I finally had the chance to audition.

The tryouts were for Slamson, the Lion, the mascot for the Kings. This was my opportunity to make it to the NBA, though it didn't go exactly the way I wanted. I ended up not getting the job with the Kings. However, the person who was offered the job was (at the time) the mascot for the Carolina Panthers, an NFL team. This left the Panthers mascot job vacant. I immediately flew out to Charlotte, North Carolina, to audition. The Panthers' job is what in the end brought me to the Southeast. Here was this tree-hugging, coffee drinking, liberal-minded guy from Seattle coming to North Carolina. In the South, I learned that the tea is sweet, the accents are thick, and barbecue is a noun, not a verb.

As soon as I stepped off the plane, I was struck by the heat and humidity of Charlotte. In Seattle, there's a lot of rain, but relatively little humidity. In the Southern summer, walking outside will cause sweat to instantly bead on your skin. It's not uncommon to have high temperatures in the upper eighties or low nineties with humidity of eighty percent or higher. Thick and muggy is an understatement. Then add thirty pounds of black fur costume ... let's just say it was quite an adjustment.

For this tryout, I had some pro mascot experience in the NFL thanks to my time with the Seahawks, which helped me obtain the position. The mascot for the Carolina Panthers is Sir Purr, a large lovable black panther with huge paws. One of his most endearing qualities is his large and shakable belly. He had one feature that wasn't so endearing, however. While I was used to having my hands covered in some way, the majority of my previous mascot costumes had feet that were athletic shoes or close to it. This was the first costume I'd encountered with paws for feet, which was something else that took some time to get used to.

The Panthers' pre-game ritual is similar to that of other NFL teams: the music is pumping, the cheerleaders enter the field, dancing into formation to create a massive human tunnel for players to run through on their way to the field for introductions.

The Panthers' Cheerleaders are called TopCats. As the music surges and excitement builds in the crowd, the TopCats form their human tunnel. Immediately, a large cannon explosion starts the mascot on his way, carrying a giant flag with flag runners flanking his sides. The music to start this all off is loud and energetic surging the crowd's emotions higher and higher.

This was my first game as Sir Purr, new costume and all. The butterflies swirled. The anticipation mounted and the sweat dripped into my eyes. I grabbed my flag and got into position. I was at the head of a triangle of flag runners and we all bounced to the beat of the music. Smoke billowed from the entrance of the tunnel and swirled around our legs. I looked back and saw the players jumping up and down, getting pumped up to enter the field. Just as the music rose to a crescendo, there was a tremendous BOOM. This was my cue to take off running with the flag through the tunnel of cheerleaders and lead the team onto the field. When I heard the crack of the cannon, I sprinted as fast as I could. I had the flag runners at my flank and the team of huge professional football players directly on my tail. My adrenaline pumped and even though the huge paws on my feet hindered my run, I pushed on as fast as I could.

Then the unthinkable happened. Approximately twenty yards into the run, the large black paw on my right foot began to slip. The hook and loop fasteners strap on the inside of the paw came undone, and the entire paw went flying through the air. I watched as it flipped end over end in the air and landed on the ground in front of one of the flag runners to my left. I was running with a kind of limp, sporting one black panther paw and one human foot covered with a white sock. At this point, I realized I should pull over so that I didn't get run over by the 300-pound linemen that were still, literally and figuratively, on my tail. The flag runner flanking my left passed me as I inched toward the side of the tunnel. One of the camera men, who I had met prior to the game, came over to help me put my paw back on. He must have grabbed it when it hit the ground after it went sailing through the air in a perfect arc.

I screamed in costume, which is a big no-no, by the way: "Oh my God! Oh my God!" The cameraman was laughing uncontrollably. I was in a panic, but in spite of myself, I started laughing as well.

Then, when I didn't think it could get any worse, it did. I had stabbed the flag pole down in the ground

Sir Purr running full speed, leading the team out of the tunnel. This photo was taken right before the dreadful "flying paw" accident.

so I could have my hands free to put my paw back on. As I struggled with the hook and loop fasteners, the top of the flag began to tilt, and all I could think was "Timber!" as the flag fell over like a Christmas tree. As I watched in horror, the top of the flag came down directly on the head and face of a TopCat. She immediately screamed "OWW" and covered her face with her pompoms. The flag's blow landed on the top of her head and one eye. I went back to screaming in costume: "Oh my God! Oh my God!"

I then repeatedly asked the TopCat: "Are you okay? Are you okay?" Her only response was to nod her head, with pompoms still securely attached to her face. Eventually, with the help of the cameraman, I slipped my paw back on. Good as new. Welcome to the Carolinas!

 **THIS WAS MY MOMENT.
I HUNG IN MID-AIR.
HOW COULD I REDEEM MYSELF?**

The show must go on. I took a deep breath and continued to the fifty yard line. The director of entertainment told me later that it was one of the funniest moments he had ever seen. This situation made me realize that in this line of work, you have to be able to laugh at yourself. And hopefully the cheerleader didn't get a black eye or serious head injury from the debacle.

I spent one and a half years with the Panthers as Sir Purr, and one of the main highlights during this time was going to the Super Bowl in 2003. The Super Bowl was in Houston, Texas, and the Panthers played the New England Patriots. The Patriots won this game; however, most people remember the 2003 Super Bowl for one thing: Janet Jackson's costume malfunction. That flash of flesh was visible for just a brief second. However, it changed entertainment forever.

Sir Purr remained one of the most beloved characters in the city of Charlotte. I performed on average over 300 appearances a year. The holidays were an especially busy time of the year. There were hospital visits, charity events, and Christmas parties for underprivileged families. The Panthers organization took it upon themselves to adopt families in need and make their Christmases special with large gift donations. A Christmas party was held at the local fire department to celebrate and reveal the gifts to the kids. This was a perfect location due to the large bays that house the fire trucks and emergency vehicles. The Panthers' Community Relations Department delivered the gifts and decorated the bays to enhance the festivities. As a surprise to the kids, Santa Purr was scheduled to make an appearance to take photos and play with the children. Prior to the start of the event, I met with my contact person and he showed me the layout and location of where everything was going to take place. The garage was empty and open, with large piles of presents for the various families. In the middle of the garage was the bright gold fireman's pole, extending from ceiling to the floor. Santa Purr was to make his grand entrance using this pole at a specific point of the party before the kids opened their gifts.

When children are asked the question of what they want to be when they grow up, a common answer is fire fighter. The thought of being brave in the face of danger, putting out fires, and saving lives is the dream of many young children. They have visions of sleeping in the upstairs portion of the firehouse to be awakened by the bell that signals a fire. Then, quickly dressing in fireman's gear, they rush over and slide down the pole to jump onto the fire truck. As a child, I had these dreams, too. Now, I could live out another childhood fantasy of sliding down a real fireman's pole into the garage! This was going to be my grand entrance. My contact thought it would be a great idea as well. He gave me instructions on how to perform this maneuver. There is a large circle of flaps surrounding the pole on the ground leading to the floor below. When you grab the pole, your weight pulls down the pole and opens these flaps in the floor to expose the garage below. The opening is large enough to fit a fireman with all of their gear. I knew that I could perform this stunt with ease. However, I was concerned that the fur paws might be slippery on the pole and speed up my descent. So, I put on the paws to practice. My grip was sufficient enough to hold my weight and I could easily control my descent to the lower level. I was thrilled, but inside my heart was pounding. I knew that most people never get the chance to do something like this. I practiced a few times with just the paws while the firemen stood below, ready to catch me and slow my progress if needed. It was not.

The party started later that evening and I was already upstairs in costume, ready to go. Santa Purr, with his large red fur coat and red cap securely safety pinned to his head, was waiting with anticipation for his grand entrance. The families were being led into the garage bays to see their piles of presents. I could hear the muffled Christmas music below with screams of joy from the children as they saw their beautifully wrapped gifts and bikes with giant bows. The emcee for the event announced that there was one more surprise before they would be allowed to open their gifts. I heard my cue, "And now, your favorite black cat is here to wish you a Merry Christmas! The one, the only, Santa Purr." I grabbed the gold pole. As my weight settled in, the flaps in the floor opened. I looked below and saw a few smiling little faces cheering in anticipation. I wrapped my legs around the pole and hung on for dear life. Since I had practiced the stunt earlier, I was not worried one bit. I slowly released the tension on my grip and started my descent. My tail was the first thing to appear from the ceiling. The costume's large feet and hoop belly easily squeezed through the opening. All was going smoothly until my head reached the opening. The back of Santa Purr's head hit the flaps surrounding the opening. The nose and side of Santa Purr's head was wedged into the pole. I was stuck!

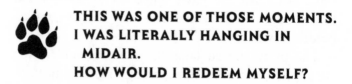 **THIS WAS ONE OF THOSE MOMENTS. I WAS LITERALLY HANGING IN MIDAIR.**
HOW WOULD I REDEEM MYSELF?

I didn't know what to do at this point. Sir Purr's costume head was fitted on the inside with a hockey helmet. Like any normal helmet, there was a chin strap. The strap inched toward my neck and began to cut off my breathing. In my head, my first thought was not to panic. I didn't want the kids below to be frightened by any sort of accident that involved the mascot. However, since I was stuck, I was not sure how to get myself free. I wiggled my body up and down to see if I could get any movement. (This must have looked hilarious from the garage below.) This didn't work. Again, I didn't want to panic, so I kicked my legs like a bicycle and slightly swung to make something happen, again to no avail. (Which again must have looked pretty crazy to the families below.) The limited air made my vision start to blur. After what felt like an eternity, I noticed the inside of the mask start to buckle. Sir Purr's face was bending in, forming a dent the size and shape of the pole. Pressure on the chin strap began to lessen and I heard a pop. (Imagine the same sound you hear when you flick your finger out of your mouth ... pop. It was like a cartoon sound effect.) Sir Purr's face warped in and I slid safely down the fireman's pole and landed on the pad below.

I am not sure what was going on in the minds of the children and families. It must have looked hysterical and horrifying all at the same time. I just simply danced around, shook my belly, and gave everyone in the party a huge hug. I did this partly as a way to do what a mascot does at appearances, which is to bring smiles to faces and pose for pictures. But also, I danced and hugged out of relief that this event didn't end up as a headline on SportsCenter.

The show must go on.

CHAPTER 8
The Pinnacle

FOR A MASCOT, working with the National Basketball Association is one of the most sought-after positions in the country. These entertainers are truly Jacks of all trades, and some of the most talented people in the world. There are performers who are acrobats, musicians, clowns, actors, and stunt men. One factor that contributes to the high quality of the performers is the fact that the NBA is all about entertainment. An NBA game can be compared to a Broadway play. The court is the stage, there is lighting, musical accompaniment, narrators or announcers, and actors or players. In some of the other professional sports leagues, the focus is entirely on the game itself. For example, in baseball, the emphasis is on the game and the entertainment is a side note. However, to the younger fan, the mascot is often at the center of the action no matter what sport it is. It was my goal to become one of these furry characters in the NBA and step into the center of attention.

I thoroughly enjoyed my brief time with the Panthers and I will never forget it. However, I felt like the NBA was my calling. The Carolina Panthers had been my ticket to the South, and the Charlotte Bobcats' mascot, named "Rufus Lynx," became my ticket to the NBA. Seeking a mascot position in professional basketball almost always means the applicant must move to a new city. Fortunately for me, an NBA mascot job opened up in my own city of Charlotte. This was my chance, and I wouldn't even have to move.

When I joined the Panthers, there was no NBA team in Charlotte. In 2002, the Charlotte Hornets had moved and become the New Orleans Hornets. This left Charlotte without an NBA team, but because North Carolina has such a strong tradition of basketball, the city petitioned for and was awarded an expansion team in 2004.

I knew that the competition for this job would be very stiff, but I had confidence. There were a number of other candidates with professional experience. A job in the NBA is often considered the pinnacle of the mascot world. Making it to this level was my ultimate goal. In September of 2005, I was offered the position of the official mascot for the Charlotte Bobcats.

I began my NBA career during the second year in the history of the entire organization. The previous mascot had stayed in the job as Rufus Lynx for one year. I knew that when I got this job, I could shape and influence the personality of this mascot character to the way I envisioned it. During the pre-season, the team continued to play in the old Charlotte Coliseum, home of the original Charlotte Hornets from 1988–2001. The new stadium was being built in uptown Charlotte and the old coliseum was scheduled for demolition.

For my first NBA game, the Charlotte Bobcats were playing the New Jersey Nets. I was determined to show the approximately 2,000 fans what they were getting in a performer. As the capacity of the coliseum was about 24,000, it was definitely not a packed house. The preseason is often seen as the testing ground for all aspects of the game, from players to entertainment teams, and our organization was no different. This was my first game in the old coliseum in front of real NBA fans. Even though it wasn't a sell-out, to me it was big time! I was the rookie, and this was my moment.

I wanted to showcase all of my dancing skills, athletic ability, and creativeness. In my mind, tumbling was definitely on that night's docket. When a time-out was called, I jumped into action and ran onto the court. One thing that I should have taken into consideration was that my personal costume hadn't arrived yet. The costume I was wearing had been designed and measured to fit the previous performer; it was not quite the best fit for me. This was my first NBA game, so I wasn't going to let that stop me. The music was jamming and the excitement of my first NBA timeout was coursing through my veins. About mid-court, I decided to throw my round off, back handspring. As I began to put my hands down for the round off portion of the tumbling pass (this is where you are supposed to execute a type of cartwheel and at the end your legs come together to hit the ground at the same time.) During the cartwheel, my body was in an upside down, with my weight on my outstretched arms and my head close to the floor. That's when it happened. My full body, including my head, continued on with the stunt. But Rufus' head

Center Court: Rufus Lynx! The name Rufus Lynx comes from the scientific classification name for a Bobcat. Species: Lynx rufus.

didn't. The most unthinkable accident for a mascot at any level occurred: I lost my head! All the times in my life that my dad had told me "You'd lose your head if it was not attached to your body" instantly became real. I know he was looking down on me, laughing his head off. Rufus' head was sitting at center court all by itself. I heard an audible "OOOHHH" as the crowd reacted in surprise, and then some laughter. To hear that small crowd in the massive Coliseum was in itself an impressive feat. I could not believe this had happened!

I own videos of ESPN highlights where mascots have lost their heads in games. One of the funniest moments, in my opinion, was when a large purple dinosaur popular with the toddler crowd lost his head during a mascot soccer game. Then the other mascots proceeded to use his head as the ball and kicked it down the field and into the goal. This was fantastically funny for the fans. In my mind, this was one of those moments. I was going to end up on an ESPN highlight reel—and not in a good way.

I ran and grabbed Rufus' head and attempted to slam it back over my head. The neck flaps folded up into Rufus' head, covering my face under the mask, which rendered me blind. I didn't care. I just continued off the court toward the entertainment tunnel. Miraculously, I made it back to my locker room without running into the stands or falling on my face. My assistant followed close behind. I pulled off Rufus' head in disbelief.

THIS WAS THE MOMENT AGAIN.
I HUNG IN MID-AIR.
HOW WOULD I REDEEM MYSELF?

My assistant was quick on his feet and said, "Dude, I'll go get some athletic tape!" I knew exactly what he was thinking, because I had the exact same thought at that precise moment. He came rushing back into the room and we immediately strapped down Rufus' head with the tape. We wrapped the entire roll of white tape around the head, under my arms and back over my shoulders. There was so much tape strapped under my arms that I could barely lower them. There was no way Rufus' head was coming off now. I took a deep breath and was back on the court the very next time out. I gingerly walked around the arena waving and acting like I could not pull off my head. My new bosses and even a few players sitting on the bench saw me and could not stop laughing. The crowd ate it up, and I believe I gained the respect of some local fans that day.

The show must go on.

CHAPTER 9
Broken Paw

I **KNEW THAT IN A** professional mascot's career, there was a good probability of serious injury. One performer who has endured more than one serious injury is the original "Hugo the Hornet," Michael Zerillo. During his career, the number of injuries and medical procedures he underwent became legend among the mascot community. When all was said and done, he had a grand total of sixteen surgeries and medical procedures. I knew that the possibility of injury was always there, especially with the trampoline dunks that a majority of the mascots in the NBA were known for. This high-flying dunking requires the character to jump off a mini trampoline positioned near the free-throw line, sending him flying through the air toward the goal, hopefully dunking the basketball and landing safely on his feet in the process.

This was a skill/stunt that I was learning to perform in costume. Since I didn't have a gymnastics background, this stunt was not really my forte. However, I was athletic enough to learn how to pull off a few tricks. My successes included "between the legs," passing the ball from one hand under the leg to the other hand while in the air, then dunking the ball; "Reverse," hitting the trampoline and twisting your body in the air to dunk the ball backwards; and "360", hitting the trampoline and rotating 360 degrees in the air before dunking the ball.

I was slowly progressing with my skills. However, my progress was hindered due to my lack of vision

Dunking at NBA Jam Session during NBA All Star Weekend as Ronald watches in anticipation.

Final dunk over the Lady Cats dancers.

in the costume. I looked through the eyes of the character, which were covered with sunglasses. The view in the mask was a kind of tunnel vision, and my peripheral vision was completely cut off. The glasses continually fogged, and my view was slightly distorted due to the mirrored plastic frames. Even with my limited vision, I was determined to make progress in my dunking ability and accomplished some of these tricks in games.

However, I was still working on the flip dunk, which is exactly what it sounds like: the mascot runs, hits the trampoline, executes a flip in the air, then dunks the basketball before landing under the goal. I was able to complete the flip dunk in practice out of costume. However, I was still working on getting it consistently in costume. A rule that I followed was that if I could make seven out of ten dunks in practice, then I could perform that particular trick at a game.

The Miami Heat were in town for a game during the regular season. During this game, we were scheduled to dunk. The dunk team consisted of a rag tag group of three dunkers and myself. I felt great and had lots of energy. For my first dunk, I slammed a one-handed windmill. This stunt consists of hitting the trampoline and while you're flying through the air, swinging the ball with one arm down and around in a circular motion like a windmill, then slamming the ball into the net. When I came down and hit the crash mat, I landed on my knees. I put my hand down to catch myself, and my fingers bent back ... CRACK! I felt a pop. I jumped up and ran back to the other end of the court to get ready for my next dunk. I noticed I couldn't grip the ball very well, and I felt a popping in my hand when I tried to hold on to it. I was so full of adrenaline that the pain hadn't set in ... yet. I knew something was wrong, but ...

The show must go on.

I was having trouble holding the ball with one hand, so I decided to do a two-handed slam. I sprinted down the court, hit the trampoline and somehow managed a two-handed dunk. I instantly ran off the court, because I knew after landing on the mat that something was definitely wrong. I thought my hand was possibly broken. I went back to my locker room, took off my head, and peeled off my costume glove. The pain was starting to set in. I told my assistant: "Go get the medic or something!" The medics came in to check out my hand and brought me some ice. I

The NBA has fans all over the world, including China. I wanted to capture something "great" at the Great Wall!

told them that I thought I had broken my hand. They told me to keep the ice on my hand, and one of the medics went to get the team doctor.

The team doctor was someone who had been working with the original Hornets in the nineties and was re-hired when the Bobcats came to town. He had personally performed some of Michael Zerrillo's surgeries in the past, making him familiar with mascots and their propensity for injury. He came into the room and examined my hand, pressing on the area, and couldn't determine any breaks due to my lack of pain response. (My adrenaline had apparently not worn off as of yet.)

His exact words were, "Oh wow, what do we have here? Hey Rufus … you'll be fine … I'll get you some warm milk and catnip and you'll be all better." (He spoke in a manner similar to when you hear someone talking to a kitten.)

My response: "I think something is seriously wrong and I may have broken it."

The doctor replied, "Okay, well, if it's going to make you feel better, let's take you down to get an X-ray of your paw."

In the training room of the arena, there was an X-ray machine. My hand continued to throb while he put it into position for the X-ray. When the result came back, the doctor was shocked. "Oh my gosh! You have a clean break in the third and fourth meta-carpel on your right hand." He paused and began to apologize, "Hey, I am so sorry for what I said to you earlier; I didn't think that it would be broken."

This made me feel a little better, but the pain was throbbing for real now. I went back to my locker room, got out of costume, and left in the ambulance, headed to the hospital to get a cast. And not a little cast, either. It left my fingers exposed and went up all of the way up to my elbow. I was devastated. We had a game the day after next, and I was scheduled to perform.

 **THIS WAS MY MOMENT.
I HUNG IN MID-AIR.
HOW WOULD I REDEEM MYSELF?**

Bringing Sexy Back *dance with the Lady Cats.*

I had to figure out how I was going to perform for the next game. I wasn't going to be able to do any stunts. How could I make that clear to the fans and still keep them entertained? I came up with a plan. To start with, I requested to have Rufus placed on the team injured list in the program. I attached hook and loop fasteners to the end of the cast near my fingers. I then cut off the fingers of one of my costume gloves and affixed them to the hook and loop fasteners. The arm fur was situated so it was impossible to tell that there was a cast underneath the costume hand and arm. I dressed in a normal suit with costume feet, costume hands, and costume head.

To complete my look, I made a pre-game visit to the vet and picked up two plastic dog cone collars. You know—those clear plastic cones that prevent cats and dogs from licking or bothering an injury. I connected the two collars together to fit my neck under Rufus' head. Then I put my broken arm in a sling over the suit. Injured Rufus costume complete!

The show must go on.

Rufus officially listed with Gerald Wallace on I.R. (Injured Reserve).

CHAPTER 10
The Final Act

I **N 2014,** the Charlotte Hornets name officially returned to the Queen City. The fans of Charlotte unanimously voted to change the name and identity of the team from the Bobcats back to the Hornets. This meant that Rufus Lynx retired, and the beloved Hugo the Hornet made his return.

Personally, I was at the point in my career that I was looking for a change. I had performed as Rufus the mascot for the previous nine seasons, and I decided it was time to hang up the fur. The community relations department had started a new literacy initiative and because of my background in education, I fit perfectly into this role. I wanted to focus more on my family and spend time with my growing daughter. I had already missed too many dance recitals and monumental events in my child's life, and I didn't want to miss any more.

For the last game of the season, my boss asked me if there was anything special that I wanted to do. He knew that this was going to be my last game as the team's mascot. I told him that I wanted to dress my daughter, Lacey, in costume as Mini Rufus and

Prior to my final game as Rufus ... Game day staff presented me with a signed, framed photo collage. It was a very special moment.

Having my wife and daughter share my retirement game with me is something that I will remember for the rest of my life.

The perfect way to end my career on court with my daughter, Lacey as "Mini Rufus".

perform a skit with her. She was seven years old, and we had an orange fur costume that showed her face but covered the rest of her body, just like Rufus. She was precious.

This was *our* moment.

I ended my career performing with my daughter on court. It was one of the best moments in my life. I was so proud of her. My wife was courtside and watched the whole skit, with tears in her eyes.

Lacey, the light of my life.

CHAPTER 11
Belayed Gratification

LIFE AS A professional mascot was crazy, fun, challenging, sweaty, exhausting, and most of all, fulfilling. As a costume character, I had the opportunity to bring a little joy to people's lives. I made them laugh and provided a bit of an escape from their own personal rat races when they attended a game. I made them laugh and provided a bit of an escape from their own personal rat races when they attended games or saw me in the community. Through my years in costume, I realized that the influence a mascot has on the lives of children is far reaching. This was something that I took tremendous pride in.

This remained my goal as I moved forward and transitioned to a new role in the department of corporate, social responsibility for the Charlotte Hornets (CSR department—some teams refer to this as community relations department).

My unorthodox career as a mascot didn't always go the way I intended. Events and moments didn't quite play out the way I envisioned. I finally realized that in most aspects of life, this is usually the case.

If I could just take a minute, breathe, and not take myself too seriously, I usually found a solution. I figured out that I just need to be patient, work hard, and eventually the fur will fly my way.

NOW, THIS IS MY MOMENT. I AM NO LONGER HANGING IN MID AIR. MY DELAYED BELAY IS COMPETE AND MY FEET HAVE FINALLY TOUCHED THE GROUND. I'VE REDEEMED MYSELF MANY TIMES AND REACHED MY ULTIMATE DESTINATION. NOW, THE SKY IS THE LIMIT.

Tail as old as time! Mascot married a cheerleader.

CPSIA information can be obtained
at www.ICGtesting.com
Printed in the USA
LVHW091441150719
624126LV00001B/41/P